# SCIENCE OF DESIRE

# SCIENCE OF DESIRE

Erin Murphy  *Erin Murphy*

*Word Press*

For Patrick, with great
admiration for your own
words and appreciation for
your efforts in organizing
our NoHo reading.
All the best,
Erin
5/8/05

Published by Word Press
P.O. Box 541106
Cincinnati, OH 45254-1106

Typeset in Baskerville by WordTech Communications LLC,
Cincinnati, OH

ISBN: 1932339515
LCCN: 2004101972

Poetry Editor: Kevin Walzer
Business Editor: Lori Jareo

Visit us on the web at www.word-press.com

Cover art: detail of "Cage" © 2004 Belle Hollon (oil on canvas)
Author photo by Leo Heppner © 2004

**ACKNOWLEDGMENTS**
(in order of appearance)

"Itinerary," *The Georgia Review*
"June 23," *Paterson Literary Review*
"Everyone Has a Story," *Pennsylvania English*
"ZipCodeMan," *Poetry Flash*
"Keene, New Hampshire, 1974," *Ellipsis*
"Satellite," *America*
"In Santiago Atitlan," *Red River Review*
"A Thing to Love," *Nebraska Review*
"The Lovers," *Comstock Review*
"Science of Desire," *The Georgia Review*
"Allen Ginsberg, 1926-1997," *Nebraska Review*
"Dear Jim," *The Lucid Stone*
"Better Than Sex," *The Lucid Stone*. This poem will also appear in the
        anthology *It's All Good* published by Manic D Press.
"A Case for the Hubble Space Telescope," *Dogwood Journal of Poetry &
        Prose*
"Not Yet Named," *Literal Latte*
"Descartes's Lover," *Field*
"Studies," *Red River Review*
"Proud Flesh," *Pennsylvania English*
"Birthday Poem," *Dogwood Journal of Poetry & Prose*
"Elegy," *Yankee* magazine

**AWARDS**

"Studies" was nominated for a  Pushcart Prize
"Not Yet Named" received 2nd Place, *Literal Latte* Poetry Awards
"June 23" received 2nd Place, Allen Ginsberg Award
"Elegy" received Honorable Mention, *Yankee* Poetry Awards
"ZipCodeMan," National Writers Union Poetry Award

**AUTHOR'S NOTE**

I wish to express appreciation for the support I have received from my family, friends, colleagues, the Dorset Colony, and the Maryland State Arts Council.

# CONTENTS

IV.

# I.

## ITINERARY

When you're having your hip replaced,
decades later, the drug they'll give you—
the one that relieves memory,
not pain—will make you think,
*This is what it must have been like*
*to be born.*

They'll name you Charles or Richard
or Margaret or Laura.

You won't find out for years
it took thirty-six hours
and you nearly killed your mother.
Don't expect her to tell you this
exactly. You'll know by the way
she tugs your hair as if to say,
*You're beautiful* and *You need a haircut*
at the same time. By then
you'll have issues of your own
that will make you flinch
when she tells you about the lump
in her breast. *Anywhere else,*
you'll think, *anywhere else.*

Your father, meanwhile, will be
the same shadow you've always watched
from the backseat as he looks
left, then right, then left again,
or from the hallway as he sits
on the bed's edge, stretching
his socks up to his knees
only to roll them down to his ankles.
When you're his age,
you'll put your son on your lap
and notice the sweater he's wearing,
the one your mother knitted

before she died, before she had
any reason to believe you'd marry.

In the first grade, you'll have
one traumatic experience:
you'll wet yourself at recess,
or walk down a crowded street
and reach up for your mother's hand
only to take hold of a stranger's.
It's why you don't trust yourself,
a therapist or a lover will insist.
During your first sexual experience
you will think, *This is my first*
*sexual experience*, and nothing else.
You won't know your last is your last.

Someone will die—a cousin,
a friend, a piano teacher.
Later, when you've outlived
most of your friends, and even
some of your friends' children,
people will go the way of lost socks.
They will be vaguely missed.

Over the years, you'll have
intimate conversations with people
whose names escape you.
You'll answer *fine* many times
when you don't mean it.
You'll wonder why the doctors
never told you you'd remember
the sounds: the piercing
of drills, the pounding of marrow.

In London—yes, you will
make it to London—you'll peer
into a closed bookstore and see
the remains of a final celebration:
half-empty bottles of Guinness,

scraps of cheese and bread.
Recovering from the surgery, you'll realize
the burden of business is not unlike
the burden of the body, the weight
of saying, *This is mine.*

**II.**

## JUNE 23

The day I was born
55 people were killed,
130 injured in a soccer game
stampede in Buenos Aires.
A continent and a day away,
something less than a stampede:
only my mother's teenage sister
comes to see me home
from the hospital. One photo
shows my mother taking a picture
of Aunt Sheila holding
the swaddle of me
in front of my parents' brick
apartment building. Who snapped
this postmodern family
portrait? A neighbor?
An anonymous passerby?
Certainly not my father
who was inside, immobile,
after knee surgery. Aunt Sheila,
in her Bermuda shorts
and thick cat's eye glasses,
looks like she is rehearsing
for a role. She is thinner
than I've ever seen her
except for the months
after the accident.
My mother wears
an inadvertent grin
as she squints us into focus,
forgetting for a moment
the practiced closed-mouth smile
that hides the teeth she hates.
Seventeen years from now
she will have them
plucked from her gums

and replaced with
straight white dentures,
and I will drive her home
from the oral surgeon's office,
her mouth packed with wads
of bloody gauze. She will
keep the pain to herself.
The day this photo is taken,
my aunt is thinking
someday she will have
children of her own.
My mother is thinking
she can change my father.
All around her are seeds
of future resentments:
for her parents who aren't here,
for my father's string of injuries
that will keep him unemployed for years,
for his family who will tell her
the divorce is her fault,
for the daughter who will say
*Leave me alone, this is my life,*
the way daughters will
before they have children—
and resentments—of their own.

## PERFECT

A number is *perfect* if it equals
the sum of all its divisors, as in 6 = 1+2+3.

> My grandmother, who hated math,
> fed her family on her husband's factory wages:
> 6 servings = 1 pound beef + 2 onions + 3 potatoes.

The first known record of perfect numbers
is Euclid's *Elements*, a surprise to those
who label it a geometry book.

> My grandmother, who wore an apron all day,
> even during dinner, filled the center pocket with nails
> one weekend and built a wall down the middle
> of the bedroom my mother shared with three brothers
> in their Euclid Avenue row house.
> *A girl needs her own room,* she said,
> handing her only daughter a bucket of paint.

The mathematics chair at the University of Illinois
was so proud of his department's discovery
of the 23rd Mersenne prime, a perfect number construct,
that he ordered the postage meter changed to stamp
$2^{11213} - 1$ *is prime* on each envelope.

> My grandmother, who never went to college,
> used a paring knife to whittle words and pictures
> into Styrofoam trays from packaged meat.
> She'd dip her designs in a saucer of ink
> and stamp them onto heavy paper
> for birthdays, anniversaries, Easter.
> Her last creation said, *Here's 2 You*
> under a scratchy outline of clapping hands,
> a graduation card for my sister, who majored in math.

## EVERYONE HAS A STORY

This is my grandmother's:
She is squeezed in the center of a convertible,
a 1934 Ford coupe, let's say—
red, like her mother's hair that whips
around in the passenger seat beside her.

The driver calls her mother *Vi*,
not *Viola*, and uses all the *v* words
he can muster. *My vivacious violet*,
he croons, then points to the Berkshires:
*a verdant view.* Asked if he's thirsty,
he answers with a deliberate *very*
as if it's the cleverest thing a man
has ever said. Her mother laughs,

the first sign, perhaps, of the looming
betrayal, like the girls who banish
one of their own, then giggle loudly
from swings across the schoolyard
to show the exiled one what she's missing.

*Mr. Wey* is how he's introduced
to my grandmother when he arrives
to take them for ice cream
and a drive in the country.
Surely not all the *gentlemen callers*
are villains straight from dime-store comics.
One, at least, must kneel down
to ask about her birthday
or to offer a teddy bear with a plaid bow
around its neck. Surely they don't all steer
with one beefy arm slung over the wheel
the way this man does as he winds
along the back roads of western Massachusetts
before cutting the engine
in front of a small brown house.

My grandmother is told to wait in the car.
*Back in a jiff,* her mother says
as Mr. Wey takes another swig
from the bottle in the paper bag
and tells her to decide what kind of ice cream
she'll get on the way home.

The story doesn't end when her mother
and the man stagger out and announce
they've just been married. It doesn't end
with the forgotten peach-flavored ice cream.
It doesn't end when my grandmother
tip-toes around him evenings
as her mother works split shifts
at the factory, or when, four years later,
he falls asleep in the green tweed chair
and never wakes up. It doesn't even end

with the small insurance check
that pays for her first pair of new school shoes.
When my grandmother learns years later
that Mr. Wey wasn't just another caller
but the real father she'd never known,
the story is just beginning.

## CONFESSION

*A woman who called the parents of a missing girl
and claimed she might be their long lost daughter
was charged Wednesday with committing a cruel hoax.*
— Associated Press

What can I say about my own family
except that living with foster parents
feels like talking to somebody
who keeps checking his watch.
They weren't cruel, nothing like that.
They fed me plenty and bought me dolls—
not real Barbies but the hollow kind
with the arms and legs that keep
snapping off and getting lost.

I'm not a bad person, really, like when I see
a mother squatting down to take a picture
of her family, I always offer to take it for her.
There's this split second when she gives me
a look like, *What do you want from me?*
But then she hands me the camera—
trusts me with it, you know—
and shows me what button to push.
It's the right thing to do—I mean,
why's there always gotta be somebody left out?

That girl was gone for so long.
Even if they'd found her, she wouldn't be
the same little 6-year-old who went missing
playing hide 'n' seek, anymore than I'm
that girl who played with broken Barbies.
Life kind of chips away at you, you know,
turns you into somebody else
with the same name.

Would it have been so terrible if they'd believed it?
There'd be a parade through downtown

and a barbecue in the park. We'd go
on "The Today Show" for sure because
I've loved Katie Couric ever since her husband died
and she was so strong, like a brave cheerleader.
After all that, we'd settle into visits for birthdays
and Christmas and Easter—I've always wanted
to come from a town where you
get dust on your shoes walking home from church.

Who would have gotten hurt, anyway?
If you'd have heard her daddy's voice,
the way it shook when he said, *Shannon?*,
you'd have told him whatever he needed to hear, too.
I mean, Jesus as my Savior, we're all waiting
for a phone call like that, aren't we? Aren't you?

## IF YOU'RE A GIRL, SAY, 13 YEARS OLD

living in a vinyl-sided townhouse
just like every other vinyl-sided townhouse
in southern suburbia except for the master bath option
where others have a his & hers walk-in closet,
you may have a best friend whose bedroom wall
borders yours so that late at night
when the world is quiet save for the laugh-track
from "Barney Miller" re-runs (*Barf!*)
you can *rap...rap-rap-rap* the secret code
that means *Meet me at the window,*
and there with your faces pressed to the screens,
talk comes even more freely
than it does in the undiscriminating light
of a summer day when you ride your bikes
to the Safeway to buy a log of Pillsbury
ready-made chocolate chip cookie dough (*Wicked good!*)
to eat raw on the curb out front, forbidden
like the copies of *Cosmopolitan* that teach you
that an ounce of sperm (*Gag!*) has 160 calories,
159 more than the can of lemon-flavored Diet Pepsi
you'll get from the soda machine at the pool
where Corey the lifeguard (*Total 'throb!*) knows you
both by name (*He likes you...No, no, no—he likes you!*),
which sends you into a giggling fit until your mother
warns from the hallway and you scurry back
under the sheets and swear that you will
let your own children stay up as late as they want
(*Swear to God!*) because before you've settled
on a butter-cream vinyl model
with the bay window and breakfast nook,
before you've uttered the words
*Do you have any idea what time it is, young lady?*,
midnight is your other best friend,
your one-way ticket to what comes next.

## A GOOD DAY

at Chicken Out means her uniform
is grease-free and pressed when she wakes up
and it's nice outside—but not so nice
that she thinks about the kids at the river
with their six-packs and suntan oil.
A good day means Carl, the manager trainee,
doesn't make her measure each order of fries
and Eddie the cook doesn't try to feel
her up when she empties the trash.
On a good day, his are the only hands
she fears.

When Billy, the other cashier, makes a joke
about her feet being *big as surfboards*,
she has the right retort at the ready on a good day:
something about her shoe size and his I.Q.

Customers say *please, thank-you*,
and *Take your time, I'll wait* on a good day,
and at least one in a suit takes off his sunglasses
when he orders as if to say, *I'm entering your world
and I don't mind*. On a good day she has time
to sit outside on a concrete picnic bench
during her soda break and imagine
that man in the suit swooping down
from the office building next door to carry her away.

Sunburned girls in cut-offs and topless Jeeps
throbbing with rock 'n' roll don't come
to the drive-thru on a good day. And because
they don't come—because, in fact, on this day
only poets have the luxury of boredom—
they can't spin off down the road
of infinite possibilities. They can't leave
in their wake a trail of giggles that say,
*Girl, there aren't words for all the things you miss.*

## THE PACER

Where to begin? Maybe
at the AMC dealership
where my pink flip-flop
scores the gravel
and my father's girlfriend
leans into the car
in her Indian print skirt,
bracelets stacked to her forearm
like a Slinky. Or perhaps
with the ride there
in the blue Rambler he'd trade,
the one with the rope tied
through front and back windows
to hold the driver's side door
closed. Or with the movie,
twenty years later,
in which the car is so uncool
it's cool again, reclaimed
like bell bottom jeans
or Pabst Blue Ribbon beer.
Or with my mother's face
that tightens when she asks,
*What'd he use for a down payment,*
*this month's child support?*
Maybe I should start
with the long ride home
in the fishbowl on wheels,
as unlikely as a bumblebee
in flight, the girlfriend's hand
on the back of my father's neck,
bracelets jangling like loose
change, and me in the backseat,
face pressed to a window
that lets in so much light
but no air.

## THE NEWS

A man in a gray suit and glasses
saying *technicality* and *never mind.*
And before this, hushed voices
in our kitchen, my friend's mother

telling mine *I don't want to have to
explain 'erection.'* And before this,
running into Lisa Saturday morning
at a downtown department store—

the one with the spiral staircase
and brass elevator doors—where
our mothers keep us apart, saying
we shouldn't speak until after the trial.

And before this, the policeman at my house
with mugshots in a padded blue photo album
like so many on our family room bookshelf.
And before this, finishing her brother's

evening edition paper route as if nothing
has happened, as if a pale naked man
in a red muscle car has not just
called us over and told us to get in,

*just get the fuck in NOW.* And before this,
believing *exhibitionist* is a good word—
like something an artist does—
and not even knowing the word *rape.*

And before this, the satisfying *thud*
of each newspaper's tight missile
landing on doorsteps as afternoon sunlight
unravels the loose narrative of leaves.

## KEENE, NEW HAMPSHIRE, 1974

My grandfather who does not touch his wife
fashions a make-shift nest for a baby swallow
marooned under a red-leaf maple.
The bird is hurt and the mother is gone.
Its heart beats *fast fast fast*
like someone frantic for an answer.
My grandfather finds a basket
in my grandmother's craft closet
and scoops the bleating bird into a bed of grass.
He ties his work to the tallest branch
he can reach from a ladder wedged
against the trunk. I watch from the sandbox
and, later, from the kitchen window
as he busies himself with yard chores,
one eye always on the tree. He wears
the closest thing to casual he's ever owned:
a thin undershirt with khaki shorts,
hard-soled dress shoes and white socks
stretched to the knees. At the kitchen table
my grandmother teaches me to make dog magnets
with bone-shaped biscuits and black felt.
Years later, at her hospital bedside,
my grandfather's words *I love you*
will be more alarming than her illness.
I don't remember if the swallow survived.

## ZipCodeMan

You tell him your five digits
and he tells you your town—
any state, any country,
even the moon, if the moon
had a post office, so the people
on this mid-western street corner
toss out numbers like horseshoes:

*02859!*

*Pascoag, Rhode Island,*

*21911!*

*Rising Sun, Maryland—*
*and by the way, Buck's diner serves*
*the best crabcakes in the state,*
he says and I glance over at my brother
who came here for college
a decade or so ago and took
the scenic route to a degree
and to this girl at his side,
the one with scrapbooks
of Europe and a Rubbermaid tub
stocked with craft supplies,
the one who is so different
from my brother who put off
writing his 5th-grade autobiography
until the night before it was due,
watching as my mother and I
skimmed frantically through photo albums,
looking for pictures of him
and finding only a few, second-child
syndrome—all of my parents'
enthusiasm for first teeth and steps and bikes
used up on me, but not, for some reason,

on a wooden door I'd never seen
before, a photo of which was
preserved in a sleeve as if it mattered
to someone, so we glued it on
the last page of his project,
with the line, *And this is the door
to my future*, which struck just
the right corniness nerve in his teacher,
who rewarded him with an *A*
and all he ever needed to know
about procrastination and letting
women do his work for him,
not that I am thinking about this
now, as my brother calls out
*91659*, the zip code for the remote
Alaskan village where he and my mother
lived when I chose boarding school
over 60-below temperatures and where
my 5'6" brother hunted bear
and caught salmon and was the tallest
player on his basketball team
and where I, brimming with hormones,
visited once and rode on the back
of a snowmobile driven by an Eskimo
boy named Ronnie who was
handsome enough to make me
want to forget my roommate
and my all-girl classes and the
production of *Hello Dolly* in which
I was to play the teary Ermengarde,
to forget all of that, until my mother
put me back on the plane,
an Eskimo shotgun wedding
not what she had in mind for her
only daughter, who is, at this moment,
thinking that maybe I haven't ever
committed myself to much of anything,
either, too eager to ride whatever
wave came along, not like ZipCodeMan,

so disciplined, so thorough,
even now as he pinches his temples
and squints at my brother, saying
*Not Bethel, not Platinum, not Goodnews*
*Bay,* unable to name the exact
Alaskan village, population 78,
and feeling like a failure, his life's work
unraveling right in front of
the Friday-night after-dinner crowd,
his bread and butter, while my brother
grins just a little, just enough to show
he's proud to stump up this man who
can tell us so much about where we've been
but knows even less than we do
about where we're going.

## OFFERING

Each afternoon as he pulls out
of the parking lot on his motorcycle,
his part-time handyman work done
for the day, the office ladies shudder,
their way of crossing themselves
for the boy who puts up shelves
and hauls off garbage and laughs
when they call him *Peach Fuzz*.

Now he's dead. Betty has heard this
from Sandy in human resources
who heard it from his younger brother
who sounded *so brave* when he called.
Something about an electrical
accident, a swimming pool,
and now the news jolts through
the office to the computer stations
where the ladies reconcile
numbers with other numbers.
Someone mentions flowers,
a card. A collection is started.
They think of neighbor boys
who cut their lawns.

When he walks in the next day,
shrugging off his brother's prank
as easily as he sheds his leather jacket,
they hand him the envelope
stuffed with cash. The boss says,
*Now you know how much
you're worth to us* and tells him
to buy a copy of *Tom Sawyer*.
There is a giddiness, like
when the power goes out
in a crowded restaurant.
And the boy, too young

to know grief or love, offers
to buy everyone lunch.

## SATELLITE

You could see it best
from the marsh out back,

the satellite your father spent
his career constructing.
Evenings after dinner he took you

out to watch it sift
in and out of clouds the way

a dolphin parts the waves,
then disappears again
beneath the surface.

It was almost a star
with its subtle pulse

that left it quivering between
fullness and the outline
of a solitary zero.

Every night he told the same
story of its birth

as you measured the steady logic
of its westward course.
When he spoke you could see the rhythm

of his breathing as his shoulders
lifted, then fell, and you watched

his eyes blink slowly,
never closing all the way
but never really opening.

## SISTER SUBJUNCTIVE

It should be the name of a flower:
*Anorexia*, from the Greek *anorexis*,
a leggy variation of the daisy
with soft, yellow perennial petals.

This should have been a letter.
But it was as if the thing that consumed
you were a remote third-world country
where you could not be reached.

Your last meal here should have been
pasta with clams, black olives, hearty
stewed tomatoes, red wine and the pungent prose
of garlic bread. It was water with a rice cake,

thin and brittle like the fists
I should have cupped in my thick palms.

## MURMUR

my grandfather's heart skips a

beat

it has since he was just

small

his twin died at fifty

three

my grandfather holds his

chest

when he walks fast as

if

he can keep his heart on

track

I once took his pulse

by

holding my finger to his

wrist

I felt the missing

beat

the bird with the broken

wing

the voice that trails off mid

thought

## IN SANTIAGO ATITLAN

There is a slow creaking like bedsprings
or a swing, and then the dock
folds in on itself like a *v*
with me at the center, and the bodies
pour into the lake's muddy, sucking bottom.
I wave my passport above water
as if making a bid, thinking,
if it's ruined, I will be pinned
under this dock forever.

*** 

*Like bedsprings*, I say
because we're in bed now
where the phrase *worst experience*
buoys our intimacies.

*** 

It isn't easy to say *help*
in any language.

*** 

You were in New York City.
The men who wanted your wallet
were armed. You ran from them,
past the crowds on 125th Street,
past the cop on the corner,
past anyone who might
mistake you for someone in need.

*** 

I could tell you about
the time my mother—

who always wanted to be a writer—
rode fifteen floors
in an elevator with a man
who held a poised switchblade
in one hand, a bag of peanuts
in the other. The next day
she called in sick and lay
on the sofa, her knees pulled
tight to her chest. *Puzzled amusement*
is how she described
his expression when she told me
to put it in a story.
I was writing stories then.

\*\*\*

*With an expression of puzzled amusement,*
*he offered her a peanut.*

*I want to kill you, he said*
*with a look of puzzled amusement.*

\*\*\*

In Santiago Atitlan
there were no ambulances,
no lawsuits, no papers waiving
all rights and blame.
We had two hours until
the next boat back so I wandered
the town like any other tourist,
my clothes a stiff reminder
of what had happened,
my hair a dried, crusty parody
of itself. We *gringos* passed each other
in the *calles*, and this time
there was more than blonde hair
and pale skin to link us:
markings, poultices of mud

on our faces and hands.
In a leather *tienda* a man
told me he'd tried to catch me
as I went down but missed.

***

I could tell you about the time
my brother, two years old,
fell from the second-story window,
gripping the tiny Superman figurine
I'd stepped on earlier that day.
The chest was dented in
as if he were taking a deep breath.
I kept it to myself. Telling the story
now my brother always mentions
the doll whose injuries were worse
than his own.

***

*It's only a subtle departure
from the truth*, I tell myself,
like my mother's certain wisdoms
that have taken on meanings
of their own: you can cut yourself
more easily with a dull razor;
never lying means never
having to remember what you've said.

***

Perhaps the bottom of the lake
didn't suck me in at all.
Perhaps it was more like
a cushion, softer even
than this mattress. And maybe,
just maybe, there was something beautiful
about the islands of mud on my body,

40

as if I'd been waiting for it
to happen so that years later, you—
or someone else, would draw me close.

# PALIMPSESTUOUS

This is about my uncle,
my father's twin,
the child my grandparents
never knew, the one
who held Easter in one hand,
a Camel unfiltered in the other,
who, unlike my father,
dropped the *r's* in *barn* and *car*,
who shouldered his hard,
shirtless, farmer's body
against the plow
for the black & white circa 1942,
who called another *Mother*,
then married her.

This is about that woman
(step-aunt? mother? wife?)
who took pity on the parents
and later set *son* aside
to trace the sluice
of hair from his navel
down to the rim of his Levi's.

And this is about telling
the story to you, you
who will sleep in a mauve room
as long as it isn't *pink*,
you who once shook hands
with a call girl as if thanking her
for a second mortgage.

I am your lover, your wife,
the mother of your
children, your confidante:
you covet me, you covet me not.

## THEOREM

The shortest distance
between two points
is the split second
before you sneeze,
the smell of sulfur
from a spent match.
It's an arc of sunlight
teasing a kitchen window,
the jolt of a train
stopping mid-track.
It's the echo of a child
called home at dusk,
the line from a song
you think you know.
It's the memory of a girl
unraveling a knot
of sky blue panties,
a soldier frisking himself
to find if he's been shot.

## READING THE TREES

My mother wants me to write a poem
about something her husband's nephew said
the day he was released from prison.

With 19 years of hard time behind him,
he arrived at his childhood home and said,
*I can't believe how much the trees have grown.*

My mother tells me this on the phone.
Later, in the car, she repeats it
without context: *I can't believe how much*

*the trees have grown.* I think my mother
wants this to be a poem about sorrow,
about everything we miss. She wants

it to be the moment in the movie
when the audience lets out a collective gasp,
when they forgive this wayward boy

for robbing a convenience store
with a toy gun his senior year. The poem will not
mention the father my mother never knew

or the son in Seattle who rarely calls
or my own memory of wearing glasses
for the first time. It will not be a poem

about not wanting to write a poem.
The day I walked out of the optometrist's office,
I saw trees for the first time: black branches

clawing the autumn sky. Until then,
they'd been the blurred *idea* of trees,
a strong suggestion I had always followed.

## THE PROBLEM WITH MY NAME

In New England, where I was born,
they inflate the first syllable: *Air-in*.
But in the south, where I spent
my school years, classmates snickered
when teachers called me *Urine*.

In graduate school, an American professor
trilled *Erin Murphy, Ireland Potato*
and insisted I read Yeats aloud.
What did I know about sounding Irish?
I was from Connecticut, the place
newscasters are sent to shed their accents.
The closest thing to Ireland I'd seen
was the Notre Dame sweatshirt
my father wore when he showed up
wired and uninvited to my high school graduation.

Here's what people think: I'm Catholic;
I drink; I sunburn easily; I can pinpoint
on a map the county where
my great-great grandparents lived;
I'm one of 17 children;
my father, like all Irishmen,
is the good-natured life of the party.

I had an Italian boyfriend in college
who was in love with all things Irish.
I think he expected me to cook him porridge
in the morning and sing ballads
by the fire at night. He asked me to sew
a Guinness patch on his black thermal shirt,
not realizing I knew even less about sewing
than I did about Ireland. He stitched it himself
under my dorm room's florescent light,
and I knew then we wouldn't last.

*Murphy*, I told a Dungarven hotel clerk years later.
M-U-R—
He interrupted.
*God help me if I can't spell that name, Spud.*

I've considered using my middle name, *Courtenay*.
My mother blames my father for the strange
spelling, says it's after a philosopher
he read in college. I like the image
of my father in an Irish-knit sweater,
holding forth on existentialism
in the student union. It makes him seem smart.
It makes him seem sane. It makes me want
not to want another name.

## A THING TO LOVE

*after Lee Upton*

I am coming up on your image
of the man whose nose bled the first time
he put his face against a woman's breast,
and I am thinking the most I have to offer
is my sister who is too embarrassed
to eat tomatoes because they're
*so...sexual,* as she once confided to me
not on New Year's Eve or on a train,
but in a café in Boston where the mood
was ripe for quirky confession
and I found myself wanting to make up
some distinctive dysfunction of my own,
the way I once decided to love clotheslines,
not because I loved them but because
they seemed like a thing to love,
all of those disembodied limbs reaching out
like words to no one in particular.

## THE LOVERS

It was not about art,
the argument that wrenched him
from the bed, her bed,
to the front door where
he wields the leather hybrid
of briefcase and weekend bag,
committed to neither work nor play.

But, as always, it comes down
to seeing versus saying,
to the way his hand fingers
the doorknob, hers tucks under
an armpit in a makeshift
bra/embrace. Perhaps he is

remembering the time she wrote
*Don't upset the apricots*
instead of *apple carts*.
She might be thinking
of the 200 bell peppers
he cross-sectioned to find
the closest thing to a heart.

The headlights of a passing car
score his face in black and white.
The corner of her mind tilts
toward a back room where
her daughter sleeps. Any minute
the girl may appear,
all pastels, her cheeks a relief
of wrinkled sheets.

Imagine the next stroke
of luck or brush: an open door,
all sorrow ajar
in this study of life, still.

**III.**

## SCIENCE OF DESIRE

There is a fine
line between causal
and casual.
Her spaghetti strap
hesitates on her
shoulder like
an unanswered
question. He is
thinking *lingerie*
is the perfect
word: *linger*
all dolled up
in French perfume.
*Linger* with
an attitude.
*Linger* like the
finger that will
help her silk camisole
make up its mind.
Something more
powerful than
inertia is at work
here, something
more than gravity
itself, as if
Mrs. Fuller's
chalkboard eraser
never smacked
the wall or plunged
to the floor
in a cloud of dust,
as if even now,
decades later,
it's suspended mid-
air in that stale
classroom.

(*Inertia. Inertia.*
He would marry
Inertia. He would
father Inertia.)
The solar system,
too, is still
propelled by some
unspeakable momentum;
the worms continue
to sluice elaborate
threads only to have
them scraped away.
Do they weep?
Did Charlemagne,
after irreparable
damage to his ilk,
have any regrets?
Would the tightrope
walker, paralyzed
from the neck down,
have it any other
way?

Once at the Bronx
Zoo he watched
a snake slide right
out of its skin
without looking back.

He's seen grown men
leave their children.

He's familiar with
the least resilient
of all fibers.
Steamed or pressed,
it can never be reshaped:
silk has no memory.

## ALLEN GINSBERG, 1926-1997

Tonight, as poets the world over
ready words for you,
I can't even put my hands
on a copy of *Howl*, a poem
I want to share
with a 13-year-old boy
teetering between writing
and right field,
the son of the first man
I've loved since that
tectonic shift we call
divorce, and when I find it
in a bible-size anthology,
a far-cry from the pocketbook
edition I once used
to shield my heart,
we draw straws, and I
read some and he reads some
and a neighborhood boy
who hasn't seen his father
in two years reads some,
and they like that they
can say *screwed* and *faggot*
without reprimand, and they like
spewing out a string of lines
*like rap*, and the man I love now
is listening and smiling,
the terrain of his face
mapping things he won't say,
and when it's my turn again
I let loose in this linguistic striptease,
tossing out words like garters
that reverberate around
the room where chairs
should be, where a table
and shelves spilling over

with books should be, and my
very present tense lens
tells me there will be fine sex
tonight with this man
who once used chopsticks
to pluck a jelly bean
from my navel, the one
who is at this instant
cradling me from behind
in his narrow dance, whispering
in my ear that lovemaking
has its own *syzygy*,
making me feel smothered
in consonants, hungry
for the low moan of a true vowel,
now, at this intersection
of everything I've lost
and everything I think I want.

## DEAR JIM

Five years is a short time to chart
the coast of Maine in fractals,
but a long time to have the hiccups,
and so, a semi-complete catalog
of my activities since we last spoke:
I have taken charge of a non-profit
organization, which means I usually know
the difference between *fiscal*
and *physical*. I have debated shades
of gray in vinyl and learned
that *amortization* has nothing to do
with love. I've heard a husband
say *I want someone else*,
then later retract that statement,
and I've crawled under
a down comforter and moaned
about every major organ
but my heart. (Oh, about
the hiccups: please don't be
too concerned—my doctor expects
a breakthrough any year now).
I've considered making T-shirts
of my son's original sayings, including,
but not limited to, *You can't change
the past but you can always
change the channel.* By the way,
I've had a son for four out of five years.
Last August I recruited a group
of like-blinded poets to write
a Mad Lib of a Galway Kinnell poem.
Boy, wouldn't he be _____!
                                       adjective
More recently, I have wondered
about your poems and your life
and that well-tended patch of hair
on your chin. What I mean to say is,

I put my pants on one day at a time,
too. Sometimes they fit better than others.

## BETTER THAN SEX

It's not every day
that a veterinarian
gets a call about
a cat swallowing
a condom. It's not
every day that a man
stands naked in his
kitchen saying,
*Look, I said 'balloon'*
*to the receptionist,*
*but it's not a balloon,*
*it's a...a...ribbed*
*latex Trojan with*
*spermicidal lubricant.*
It's not every day that
a veterinarian has to
put down the phone
because he's laughing
so loudly that the man's
then-girlfriend/
now-wife can hear
him across the room
where she's cradling
the same cat who,
two years from now,
will be banished
to the basement when
the real baby is born.
And it's not every day
that I think about
the time when we had
afternoon trysts
instead of carpools
and late meetings,
or when—after
the condom had *passed,*

as the vet promised—
we lay in bed and laughed
and laughed and laughed
until it felt like we'd
come all over again.

# A CASE FOR THE HUBBLE SPACE TELESCOPE

*On Thursday, astronomers will crowd into
a hotel ballroom in Washington to discuss
when and how NASA should put down one
of its and astronomy's most spectacular
successes, the Hubble Space Telescope.*
—*The New York Times*, July 27, 2003

It was launched the year I first heard the phrase,
*You can't have a great job, a great apartment,*
*and a great lover all at the same time,*
a theory I believed because my man and I
had just moved to the top floor of a farmhouse
where I spent many unemployed hours
admiring the view of the Berkshires
until I finally found work at a college
where the dean named Dr. Hubbel
(*e-l*, no relation) slurped his top teeth
and most certainly was missing
the *lover* part of the equation
since he seemed to get his thrills
from eliminating positions, a fate
some government officials have in mind
for the Hubble telescope, saying it's time
to *put it down,* like Old Yeller
or the shrubs my horticulturalist neighbor
told me had *served their purpose,*
which makes me wonder when
we started killing things just because
they've lasted longer than we expected,
and, if that's the way it works, why there are
so many reality shows and poems
about looking out of windows,
things so unlike the Hubble, which,
despite its flawed-mirror birth defect,
is really pulling its load, keeping a steady gaze
like a husband who comes home on time,
outdoing what it was designed to do

in its decade-plus in the sky, which is more than
many of us can say as we make our way
to gray desks or turn keys to dark rooms
or haul our tired bodies onto other bodies,
barely looking one another in the eye,
the only part of the human anatomy
that is the exact same size at birth and at death,
an organ that spends a lifetime learning to see
what needs to be seen.

## THE WARNING THAT SHOULD COME WITH WINDOW TREATMENTS

My new neighbor thinks I can't see him
when he's naked, thinks his scrim of a shade
is sufficient, though it offers only
as much privacy as the smoky haze
of a jazz bar on a Saturday night.

When I'm washing the last of the dinner dishes,
I'll look up just as he's undressing for bed.
It's usually not much to see—he'll toss
his work jeans on a chair and pull on
a pair of boxers. Some nights, though,

he gives himself a good look in the mirror,
turning sideways and sucking in his gut.
It's a bookish kind of voyeurism: me looking at him
looking at himself and wondering
what a woman sees in a man like him.

## MY NIECE BRINGS HER CHEF BOYFRIEND TO DINNER

The one from New Hampshire kept rotweilers.
This one keeps a shift's worth of bernaise loose
with a few tablespoons of heavy cream.
So, what to feed a cook when he's at home?

I choose beef stew with whole allspice berries,
salad with homemade croutons, a baguette.
I set salt and pepper on the table,
remove them, reconsider, put them back.

I want to know if he worries sauces
like I worry words, if he eats nachos
and double-stuffed Oreos dunked in milk
the way I say *Yes, I know what you mean*

when I don't: a dash of imprecision
in this world where silence growls like hunger.

## MY FRIEND CONSIDERS MOVING
## TO A SMALL TOWN IN NORTHERN MAINE

> *Should we have stayed at home and thought of here?*
> —Elizabeth Bishop, "Questions of Travel"

*But the winters*, I say.
She doesn't care: she's never
been there but she's in love
with the idea of a new place,
new people, a house with
a built-in china cabinet.
She does her research—education,
real estate, cost of living—
and calls the elementary school
to ask if there's a pre-k program
for her son. The man who answers
says he'll have to check on it
to be sure (to be *shaw*), as he is
the janitor. That's when my friend

decides she doesn't need to move:
in her mind, she's already lived there.
She's decorated the Victorian
with the wrap-around porch,
the one on Century21.com.
She's gotten to know Maggie,
the cashier in the general store,
well enough to ask after
her brother's bursitis.
She and the kids have found
the best sledding hill
in all of New England,
nicknamed it Mt. Sledmore.
What else is there to do?

I understand. So many times
I've thought of writing

a whole series about, say,
the various definitions of *want*,
scribbling pages of notes,
then stopping before the poems
take shape. It feels as if
they're already written.

The janitor calls my friend
back 10 minutes later to say
he's sorry, there isn't
a pre-k program. I love
this man, how he wipes down
the cafeteria tables every day
after lunch, pours the pink
crystals on the first grader's
vomit. I think we've all lived
in his small town. We've all
left the basketball game
on a snowy night without
thanking him for waxing
the worn gym floor, for finding
a way, year after year,
to make it new.

## NOT YET NAMED

It's 7 p.m., snowing, and all the taxis
are taken. Judy, who prefers to be called Judith,
covers me with her red coat.
*We must protect the pregnant one,*
she says. But this isn't serious snow—
it's more like the animated flakes in the film
we've just seen about Communist China.
Belle, whose husband calls her Corinne,
strikes a cab-hailing pose while Maryke,
who has made her Dutch name more palatable
to Americans, says, *That's right—you are two.*

In the film the narrator's father was mistaken
for a spy because of his Russian name.
When he tried to hang himself,
his son clung to his feet until he fell, gasping but alive.
Belle's daughter, 9, has just read a book
in which a girl commits suicide by jumping
off a bridge. She has more questions
than her mother can answer. As a child
Maryke spent two years in a Japanese prison camp.
She stopped asking questions.

Soon we will give up on a taxi and trudge
around the corner to a restaurant that serves
only *halal* meat. Judy will explain that the cows
have been blindfolded against the slaughter
of other animals.

Spring will come, then summer,
then you. Then all the things you shouldn't see—
and all the things you should.

## TEACHING TANYA

Her vision is normal but it's as if
her eyes can't find anything
worth seeing. There are initials for it:

*TBI, traumatic brain injury,*
the shorthand needed when something
happens too often. Tanya was six,

now nine. Her school file says
*automobile accident,* speculating only
about effect, not cause.

A specialist wants to see the poems
she writes for me this week.
So far I have been lucky

if she scribbles her name on a frayed
blank page. But today I detect something
like a smile when I explain metaphors.

She curls over the paper, her marker
squeaking on the desktop like wheels
on a distant car rounding a sharp curve.

Here is what she gives me:
*Humingberd — a littel gerl
in the green gras wayves a red flagg.*

## CAESURA SECTION

*Fetal distress,* we're told
and I picture a small, curved boy
sending flares, orange
flares, against a black sky.
I'm gurneyed to the o.r.,
where my husband, all green scrubs
and nervous smiles, holds my hand
as doctors slice into me, not like a pen
scoring a page, but like
a dull hunting knife, sawing into a tough
leather baseball glove. I feel
a deep tugging, like this baby
is suction-cupped to my spine. The doctor
is pulling, prying him loose, and I am
thinking of pulling, pulling words
from my younger brother: *b-b-b-bicycle,*
*g-g-g-giraffe,* until the day
he learned to say, *Fuck you,*
*Sis,* with no sign of a stutter.
I am thinking, thinking of the angry
woman in the park, the one
who dreams, every night, of her son
sliding right out of her, *a perfect*
*vaginal birth...* am thinking
*vaginal* is close, too close,
to *virginal*—*a perfect virginal birth,*
though God, for me, is purely
rhetorical at this point, as in
*God, let this be over,*
*Jesus Christ, are we there yet?*
More pulling, more prying
and then a sputter, not like
a baby's cry, but like
an old dot-matrix printer, a long
*eh-eh-eh-eeehhhh, eh-eh-eh-eeehhh ...*
and he is fine, pissing

in the doctor's eye, the doctor
who begins to tend me, stitching
my incision that will harden, scar
like a Braille hyphen, punctuating
the before — the after
like that game, the one in which you fuse
two unrelated phrases: *Once upon a time
heals all wounds.*

## SADIE SCRUBS FLOORS IN NEO-NATAL


Even an air-born spore or patch of mold
can take hold of these babies called *micros*,
smaller than the kittens birthed by the stray
last spring in her backyard shed. Sadie sprays

odorless cleanser, wears gloves, latex-free,
as red-eyed fathers wander out for coffee
and new mothers fumble with medical terms
the way nervous tourists try foreign words.

Does she have children, they all want to know.
Four, she says, sure to include James Moses
who lived just two days. Sometimes newborns thrive
like fattened pink chickens. But other times

mothers hold babies, stripped bare, to their chests,
a communion of flesh, breath to last breath.

## DESCARTES'S LOVER

> *When a husband weeps over a*
> *dead wife...in spite of this,*
> *in his innermost soul he feels*
> *a secret joy.*
> —René Descartes

What of a father for his daughter?
She was a baby, barely
able to separate her own body

from mine. I remember
the day she discovered her nose:
she twisted it in her fist

as if uncorking a wine bottle
until—coming to accept it—
she patted it like a kitten.

She was your impossibility:
the only time one plus one
equaled one, and you

studied her the way
I've watched you study those
Dutch still-life paintings.

If you could, you'd set right
every teacup precariously
balanced, every spoon, crust

of bread, skull, pheasant,
pear, wine glass. You're troubled
especially by the red brocade

rug that fancies itself a wall,
swallowing the room's
contents—chair, map, vase,

telescope—troubled, too,
by tiny limbs restless
to hold and be held,

by wails which could mean
hunger, a soiled breech, fear.
Sickness. If you had known

her as a small child, perhaps you
would have seen that perfection
can come from things

imperfect. Perhaps you would have
teased her: *I think therefore
I'm a yam, or a ham, or a jar*

*of jam. You think therefore
you'll scram, my little apple
of the earth, if you know what's good.*

You can doubt everything:
the sweetness of honey;
a bee's sting; a pencil

bent in water; the pool
of candle wax from a night
of love; the universe

dancing around Earth,
its sullen partner; the smell
of roses wafting through

your window while you,
at noon, are still
in bed, your meditations

scattered about you
like handkerchiefs
after a night's fever.

But can you deny
a body swollen with you
to a lob-sided circle,

or the womb of sweet earth
that buried our child,
my love?

## SEVILLIAN DREAM

How I've forgotten to pick up my son
at his *escuela* I don't know,
but I'm relieved to find him
toe-tapping his soccer ball
along the banks of the Guadalquivir.
There are steps to climb, so many
of them, and it is hot, hot enough
to lose yourself in the whole process
of the body, which I must have done
because when my son hoists himself
to the top of the railing, poised
like a rare bird over the sidewalk
so far below, I don't lunge for him
the way I do on street corners, in parking lots.
There is the falling, falling and my running
down the steps, breathless, gasping.
But his landing is a surprise,
graceful and gentle, a soft echo
of my younger brother's skull-first hard smack
in that other hot city, so many dreams ago.

**STUDIES**

*In memory of C.J.*

Four million Americans have Alzheimer's disease.

       You have one father.

The neurons in the victims' brains
contain protein filaments called tangles.

       He points to his head and says,
       *I'm not okay in here.*

Those with the least education suffer
the highest rate of the disease.

       When the nurse's aide calls him *professor*,
       he lifts his head a little and smiles.

In the late stages, they forget that they've forgotten.

       You give your father his birthday gift—
       a picture of his grandson—
       and he says, *This you, I mean,*
       *then you, I mean…I don't remember*
       *what I mean.*

Ultimately, victims' pasts are erased entirely.

       You remember Friday night dinners out,
       your father proud he could afford
       shrimp cocktail all around. You remember
       him pitching, pitching, pitching to you
       in the backyard, then shrugging
       when you turned to the piano.
       You remember the way he screamed in a whiskey rage
       over your broken bike, then replaced it
       the next day, no apologies.

As her disease progressed, the novelist
Iris Murdoch liked to watch *Teletubbies*.

     Your father lies awake in a darkened room,
     his Yankees cap on his head, his hands
     crossed over his chest.

Death, when it comes, is a formality.

     Like *please, thank you*
     and *I'm sorry*.

## PROUD FLESH

My neighbor's wife calls it his *worry sore*,
like fretting can be channeled, a funnel
for a vat of acid. From over here,
the source is obvious: he was the one

who ran that stop sign. The young girl who died
was from the next town over. A decade
later, there's a traffic light, a lawsuit
settled, a tired man who is afraid

to give each step his full weight. A doctor
suggests meditation: repeat a word
over and over till it means something
else. My neighbor seems to prefer working

his garden like the day itself depends
on this season's tulips: blood-red, short-lived.

## BIRTHDAY POEM

It's 2 a.m. and I can't remember
the last name of my friend Joy
who died of breast cancer.
I can see her wig, slightly matted,
with the curls she always wanted,
see her holding hands with her daughter
that afternoon we walked to Long Point.
But the name...a *W*, I think...damn it...
Joy, who kicked her drinking husband out
the last month, who interviewed
the local politician (*no sir, tell me
what you think, not what you think
everyone wants you to think*),
who drew a thousand yellow smiley faces
and called it *Portraits of Prozac*.
Walton? Williams? Winston?
I brought her copies of *Vanity Fair* and *People*,
heated a few cans of tomato soup
in her grease-splattered kitchen.
I never took an SOS pad to that back-splash
or made a homemade stew, never
drove her, like her good neighbor did,
to the Grand Canyon, i.v. trolley in tow.
I just sat with her every few weeks
in that dark bedroom that smelled
of her daughter's new kittens,
picked up her spilled blue pills
from the carpet under her bed and ticked them
one by one into the bottle,
reaching for them the way I'm combing my mind
now for her name: Wilson? Wiggins?
The tattered paisley address book
is gone so I can't look her up
and anyone who knew her is asleep now
so I can't call—and besides,
my stepdaughter is downstairs talking

to a boyfriend an ocean away,
which is how far I feel from late-night
hushed giggles and a phone cord
stretched to the front stoop,
that is how old I am now, old enough
to have forgotten the name of a friend
who died, *died* for God's sake,
not a friend who gave me a ride
to Syracuse one weekend or loaned me
a gown for a college ball.
Her daughter lives with the ex now.
He's remarried and sober, I'm told.
Once when my husband and son
ran out of gas on Route 213,
the new wife picked them up in her red Saab
and took them to the Texaco in Galena.
She seems nice, they said. Dyes her hair.
Gwinner. Joy Gwinner. And her daughter's name
is Hope.

# THE VIEW FROM HERE

### 1. *Fan*

Splayed petals of a proud flower,
schoolgirls twirling within a fence.
My mother waving goodbye, goodbye.
Endless cartwheel, fist unclenched.


### 2. *Basket*

Boxy bonnet, congregation of braids,
inconstant vessel. This woman knows
straw's taut narrative by heart:
clasped hands, clasped hands, clasped hands.


### 3. *Clock*

Stained dinner plate in the sink,
discus I could never yield to sky.
Stern face of the man I cannot please.
Moral moon, unleavened desire.

## SITTING BESIDE MY DAUGHTER IN THE RECOVERY ROOM

her breath is the ship in a bottle
tossed by invisible waves

or the waves themselves
whispering against glass

the branches of a bonsai
swaying in a faint breeze

a finger-sized broom
sweeping a dollhouse attic

a tiny microphone
held to blinking eyes

soles of nurses' shoes
on waxed corridor floors

the miniature mountain range
sketched by an EKG

an eraser stuttering across
paper when I can't say

what comes next

## PUSHCART

My husband and I have a friend
who grew up a Russian Jew in Chicago
in the 1930s, nearly half a century
before the prize named for those real pushcarts
that lined the streets of his childhood.
He remembers peddlers in suspenders,
green and white striped awnings, piles
of fresh produce, bagels, even neckties.

Our friend couldn't come to our Chicago wedding,
so he sent his younger brother in his place.
Nikolai—Nicky—was giving up
decades of hard living to make a go
at being sober. The week after we married,
he invited us to the apartment he shared
with three Chows in the basement
of his mother's house. Tufts of dog hair
clung to the carpet, and he'd covered
the furniture with knitted throws, still tagged
with K-mart prices.

He set out someone else's idea of celebration:
a cheesecake and champagne
served in plastic flutes he had to assemble.
He watched us drink, then insisted we take
the half-full bottle home with our gifts:
two ceramic boxes wrapped only
in the importer's layered cardboard.
One was darker and slightly smaller than the other,
with inlaid mother-of-pearl. They were too similar,
really, to give together, but too different to be a pair.
Later, on the El, we realized none of it
had been for us exactly—we were messengers
charged with carrying back proof of his changed ways
to his married scholar brother.

When no one was looking, Nicky slipped
back into his old life. He died two years later.
By then, his mother in a nursing home,
he'd moved upstairs. Nearly a week
passed before they found him. I'd never heard
of a body rupturing, of organs bursting open
like over-ripe fruit, blood soaking through
mattress and box spring, through wooden floorboards
onto a dining table below.

I think our historian friend knows what it is
to be a poet. Some of us push wobbling carts
full of boiled chick-peas head-first
into bitter wind on an empty Northside street.
Others luck into a square of sun on Greenview Avenue.
Our apples are polished like memories
on a day when the whole city wants to make pie.

# IV.

## ELEGY

It could have been December that summer
afternoon at the quarry when you
sought out the shallow parts, diving
spread-eagle as if to embrace any sublimely
lying rock. I dealt with your death
for the split second after each dive
until you sprang to the surface, surprised
at your own resilience.

Who knew then that at Christmas
the gravel truck would jut out of the road
when you, swimming in whiskey,
could not avoid it? Who could splice
that August afternoon with one in winter
as if we can interchange our days
like words, as if all of life is water
washing back on itself.

Erin Murphy's poems have appeared in *The Georgia Review, Field, Nimrod, The Paterson Literary Review, Literal Latte, Kalliope,* and elsewhere. She received her M.F.A. in Poetry from the University of Massachusetts, Amherst, where she was a Poetry Fellow. Her awards include the 2003 National Writers Union Poetry Award judged by Donald Hall; a Pushcart Prize nomination; and a Maryland State Arts Council Individual Artist Award. She lives with her family on Maryland's Eastern Shore and teaches at Washington College.